D1647011

MONOGAMY

by the same author

WINNICOTT
(Collins)

ON KISSING, TICKLING AND BEING BORED
(Faber)

ON FLIRTATION
(Faber)

TERRORS AND EXPERTS
(Faber)

Monogamy

ADAM PHILLIPS

faber and faber
LONDON · BOSTON

First published in 1996
by Faber and Faber Limited
3 Queen Square London WC1N 3AU

Photoset by Parker Typesetting Service, Leicester
Printed in England by Mackays of Chatham plc, Chatham, Kent

All rights reserved

© Adam Phillips, 1996

Adam Phillips is hereby identified as author of this work
in accordance with Section 77 of the Copyright, Designs and
Patents Act 1988

*This book is sold subject to the condition that it shall not,
by way of trade or otherwise, be lent, resold, hired out or
otherwise circulated without the publisher's prior consent in any
form of binding or cover other than that in which it is
published and without a similar condition including this
condition being imposed on the subsequent purchaser.*

Parts of this book first appeared, some in different versions, in the
Independent's Saturday Magazine in January 1996.

A CIP record for this book
is available from the British Library

ISBN 0–571–17989–4

2 4 6 8 10 9 7 5 3 1

If you take in a lie, you must take in all that belongs to it.

Emerson, 'English Traits'

PREFACE

The present controversies about family values – about marriage and the divorce rate – are really discussions about monogamy. About what keeps people together and why they should stay together. About how people decide which are the important pleasures. What are couples for if they are not for pleasure? And if pleasure doesn't matter then what does? This, one could say, is the problem of monogamy.

Certainly, to talk about monogamy is to talk about virtually everything that might matter. Honesty, murder, kindness, security, choice, revenge, desire, loyalty, lying, risk, duty, children, excitement, blame, love, promising, care, curiosity, jealousy, rights, guilt, ecstasy, morals, punishment, money, trust, envy, peace, loneliness, home, humiliation, respect, compromise, rules, continuity, secrecy, chance, understanding, betrayal, intimacy, consolation, freedom, appearances, suicide and, of course, the family. Monogamy is not simply about these things, among others; but when we talk about monogamy we cannot help but talk about these things as well. Monogamy is a kind of moral nexus, a keyhole through which we can spy on our preoccupations.

For some of us – perhaps the fortunate, or at least, the affluent – monogamy is the only serious philoso-

phical question. This book is, therefore, an enquiry into
the word *we*.

MONOGAMY

NOT everyone believes in monogamy, but everyone lives as though they do. Everyone is aware of lying or wanting to tell the truth when loyalty or fidelity are at stake. Everyone thinks of themselves as betraying or betrayed. Everyone feels jealous or guilty, and suffers the anguish of their preferences. And the happy few who apparently never experience sexual jealousy are always either puzzled about this or boast about it. No one has ever been excluded from feeling left out. And everyone is obsessed by what they are excluded from. Believing in monogamy, in other words, is not unlike believing in God.

ONCE we know the rules of a game we can think about our performance, we don't have to worry about the game. We take some things for granted so that we can take other things for something else.

Infidelity is such a problem because we take monogamy for granted; we treat it as the norm. Perhaps we should take infidelity for granted, assume it with unharrassed ease. Then we would be able to think about monogamy.

PROFOUNDLY committed to the better life, the promiscuous, like the monogamous, are idealists. Both are deranged by hope, in awe of reassurance, impressed by their pleasures. We should not be too quick to set them against each other. At their best, they are both the enemies of cynicism. It is the cynical who are dispiriting because they are always getting their disappointment in first.

INFIDELITY is as much about the drama of truth-telling as it is about the drama of sexuality. It is only because of sexuality that we think about truth at all; that we find honesty and kindness at odds with each other.

The successful lie creates an unnerving freedom. It shows us that it is possible for no one to know what we are doing. The poor lie – the wish to be found out – reveals our fear about what we can do with words. Lying, in other words, is not so much a way of keeping our options open, but of finding out what they are. Fear of infidelity is fear of language.

COUPLEDOM is a performance art. But how does one learn what to do together? How to be, once again, two bodies in public, consistently together, guardians of each other's shame, looking the part? Where do the steps come from?

This is where good-looking couples can be so reassuring, inspiring even. Waylaid – as they often are – by their beauty, we can conspire, briefly, to be shameless, like them. To have nothing to hide. Good looks, after all, are our best cultural anti-depressant. They keep the show on the road.

OUR survival at the very beginning of our lives involves us in something like monogamy. Our growing up involves us in something like infidelity (we challenge our parents, we betray them, we let them down). So when we think about monogamy we think about it as though we are still children and not adults as well. We don't know what adults think about monogamy.

WE work very hard to keep certain versions of ourselves in other people's minds; and, of course, the less appealing ones out of their minds. And yet everyone we meet invents us, whether we like it or not. Indeed nothing convinces us more of the existence of other people, of just how different they are from us, than what they can make of what we say to them. Our stories often become unrecognisable as they go from mouth to mouth.

Being misrepresented is simply being presented with a version of ourselves – an invention – that we cannot agree with. But we are daunted by other people making us up, by the number of people we seem to be. We become frantic trying to keep the numbers down, trying to keep the true story of who we really are in circulation. This, perhaps more than anything else, drives us into the arms of one special partner. Monogamy is a way of getting the versions of ourselves down to a minimum. And, of course, a way of convincing ourselves that some versions are truer than others – that some *are* special.

THE only tradition we can experience is the present moment. And yet we spend most of our lives anxiously hoping we will change – looking forward to things – and doing everything we can to stop this happening. This is why we are only really relaxed, properly at ease, in periods of transition; when we can let time join in.

Infidelity is our other word for change, the only change we can know about which is a change of belief. We thrive on our disloyalty to ourselves.

THE most difficult people to be unfaithful to are one's parents. This is what makes monogamy – our capacity to find another couple – such an extraordinary achievement. Or just more of the same.

LIKE a magnet that collects our virtues and vices, monogamy makes the larger abstractions real, as religion once did. Faith, hope, trust, morality; these are domestic matters now. Indeed, we contrast monogamy not with bigamy or polygamy but with infidelity, because it is our secular religion. God may be dead, but the faithful couple won't lie down.

IF it is the forbidden that is exciting – if desire is fundamentally transgressive – then the monogamous are like the very rich. They have to find their poverty. They have to starve themselves enough. In other words they have to work, if only to keep what is always too available sufficiently illicit to be interesting.

Unfortunately, it is easier to fake obstacles – to simulate the forbidden – than to fake desire.

GROWING old together, or growing young together? There is always something to resist, something to defy.

ONE is unavoidably faithful to the dead body growing inside one. This is what makes infidelity such an irresistible conundrum, and can make monogamy seem like death.

WE are the only animals that think of ourselves as being like animals. And yet the mating habits of swans, the courting rituals of hyenas, the ants' extended family tells us nothing about our own erotic lives; nothing we can use.

Monogamy is just one of the wonders of nature. Nothing in nature is more natural than anything else.

WE may believe in sharing as a virtue – we may teach it to our children – but we don't seem to believe in sharing what we value most, our sexual partners. But if you really loved someone, wouldn't you want to give them the best thing you've got, your partner? It would be a relief not to be puzzled by this.

Perhaps this is what friendship is for, perhaps this is the difference between friends and lovers. Friends can share, lovers have to do something else. Lovers dare not be too virtuous.

WE would like there to be guidelines. We would like there to be something we could recognise – a group of people all obviously doing the same thing – that we could call monogamy. We are so hungry for reassurance, we so much need to live by the precedent of other people's lives – by quotation – that we forget how different every couple is. Infidelity sometimes jolts our memory.

IT is impossible to promise infidelity. If you are unfaithful then you have kept your word, if you are not you have broken it.

At least with monogamy your word can be your bond. Monogamy lets you keep your promise, but not always your secret.

AT the beginning of a love affair one might ask – depending on which kind of person one is: a person who prefers the future, or a person who prefers the past – What am I getting into? or, What am I getting out of? It is common sense to assume that every entrance is also an exit.

The compulsive monogamist never needs to ask these questions. This is what his compulsion is for, to convince him that the future is the same as the past. Outwitting time and change he builds a monument of continuity among the promiscuous ruins. Valuing a relationship because it lasts, he lives as if time proves something.

IN private life the word *we* is a pretension, an exaggeration of the word *I*. *We* is the wished-for *I*, the *I* as a gang, the *I* as somebody else as well. Coupledom can be so dismaying because the other person never really joins in. Or rather, they want exactly the same thing, but from a quite different point of view.

IF sexuality is for pleasures other than the pleasures of procreation, what keeps people together? What makes them stay?

Or to put it another way – the other way round – what are children if we stay together because of them? What are we asking them to be?

A couple is a conspiracy in search of a crime. Sex is often the closest they can get.

ANYONE who believes in the value of suffering, anyone who promotes pain as either a virtue or a necessity, cannot help but make us wonder whether secretly they have found a way of enjoying it. In other words, we cannot help but wonder whether they are artists, or saints – or even realists. This is why we are never quite sure if monogamy is the religion or art of the realistic or of the disillusioned.

It is difficult to tell because the disillusioned always think they are being realistic, and the realists always think they are telling the truth.

IT is not a question of what we believe, but that we believe at all. It is not a question of who we are faithful to, but that we are faithful.

Fidelity shouldn't always be taken personally.

TO describe a couple is to write an autobiography. Because we begin our lives in a couple, and are born of a couple, when we talk about couples we are telling the stories of our lives. We may try and make the couple as abstract as possible because they are so close to home. Or rather because they are home; because once there was nowhere else to live.

EXAGGERATION, in the first instance, is a way of being taken seriously; and then one is ignored for exaggerating. The reliably unfaithful, that is to say, suffer from a crisis of invisibility.

IF I am faithful she will be. But if she isn't . . .
If I am unfaithful he will find out. But if he
doesn't . . .

If I can't bear jealousy I will be her slave and her
master. But if I can I will be her . . .

If I can stop myself feeling guilty I can do what I
want. But if I stop myself feeling guilty I will want . . .

If I can keep a secret I am free. But if I need to keep
a secret I am . . .

If I have to choose I will lose something. But if I
don't have to choose I will . . .

If, but if, then . . . : the monogamist's litany.

AT its best monogamy may be the wish to find someone to die with; at its worst it is a cure for the terrors of aliveness. They are easily confused.

THERE is always the taken-for-granted relationship and the precarious relationship, the comforting routine and the exciting risk. The language won't let us mix them up. We have safety and danger, habit and passion, love and lust, attachment and desire, marriage and affairs. We are not mixed up enough. In other words, we still have bodies and souls.

AS yet, the promiscuous cannot grow old gracefully. But this may say more about our ideas of dignity, than of ageing.

WHY are so many of our fantasies of personal freedom – just like our most shameful fantasies – to do with losing control? What do we think we are? The reckless, the impulsive, the passionate are the heroes and heroines of our imaginations; the incontinent are our negative ideals.

It would be rash to assume that we are simply ashamed of our freedom, that being on our best behaviour always lets us down. That all commitment is overcommitment.

MONOGAMY comes with infidelity built in, if only as a possibility. This makes it very difficult to write about monogamy without being either cynical or naïve, without being too knowing (i.e., ironic) or too silly (i.e., ingenuous). As though you can't see it if you can't also see through it.

Writing about monogamy is like writing about sexual perversions. It is always a question of tone. The content is often a smokescreen. We should not ask, for example, is the author right, but is he bitter? And if so, what about exactly? Not, what does she believe, but what does she dread?

IF, say, you allow yourself to be more like your mother you will discover that you are different from her; if you devote yourself to being different from your mother you will turn into her. This is the first principle of coupledom. The second principle of coupledom is that you can only be like someone if you are already different from them.

CHOOSING monogamy is not, of course, choosing not to desire anyone other than one's partner; it is choosing not to do anything that violates one's idea of monogamy. Everyone flirts with their (mostly unconscious) standards of fidelity. But one is only ever really faithful to fidelity itself, never merely one's partner.

For some people it is a betrayal to dance with someone else; for other people only intercourse counts, so you can do everything else with impunity. If we didn't have our own rules how would we know we were being unfaithful? To love our partners we have to be addicted to the rules.

PEOPLE have relationships not because they want to feel safe – though they often think they do – but because they want to find out what the danger is. This is where infidelity can let people down.

ONLY the child who somewhere feels safe can take risks. Adults are less daring than children because they can never feel safe.

WHY are we more impressed by the experience of falling in love than by the experience of falling out of love? After all, both are painful, both are utterly baffling, both are opportunities.

Perhaps we value monogamy because it lets us have it both ways. It includes falling out of love as part of the ritual – encourages it, even.

THERE is a difference between not doing something because you believe it is wrong, and not doing something because you might be punished for it. One of the more bewildering things about infidelity – what can make it so morally stupefying – is that our guilty selves put pressure on us to collapse the distinction. We turn a blind eye to the difference. Tragedies are made of such forgettings, of such eagerness to please.

IN the beginning every child is an only child. The child is not possessive of the mother because he already possesses her; he behaves – in fact, lives – as if he is entitled. Our first inklings, that is to say, are monogamous ones: of privilege and privacy, of ownership and belonging. The stuff of which monogamy will be made.

Because everyone begins their life belonging to someone else – physically and emotionally inextricable from someone else – being separate, or having to share, leaves us in shock. For us, then, it is all or nothing; and so there is always potentially the feeling of being nothing that comes from not being all.

If you start life as part of someone else's body, your independence is a dismemberment. Being a couple reminds us, persuades us again, that we are also someone else; of a piece with them. As everyone who is in love (or in mourning) knows, what is politely referred to as separation is mutilation. Growing up means becoming a phantom-limb; falling in love means acquiring one.

IF sex brought us in to the family, it is also what breaks us out of the family. In other words, people leave home when what they have got to hide – their sexuality – either has to be hidden somewhere else, or when it is best shown somewhere else.

If you've got nothing to hide you've got nowhere to go. Which is one of the reasons why couples sometimes want to be totally honest with each other.

E VERY marriage is a blind date that makes you wonder what the alternatives are to a blind date.

SUSPICION is a philosophy of hope. It makes us believe that there is something to know and something worth knowing. It makes us believe there is something rather than nothing. In this sense, sexual jealousy is a form of optimism, if only for philosophers.

PARTNER, spouse, wife, husband, co-habitee. The problem of monogamy is that we have never found the words for it.

NO one is indifferent to praise; but there is no test of character like the taking of compliments. We are wary of people who are keen to be praised, because that is not what they are supposed to want, but merely what they might be lucky enough to get. No one is willing to make too great a claim for the wish to be praised, or indeed, for that talent for praising oneself that is called boasting.

But what if our strongest wish was to be praised – and so to praise – not to be loved, or understood, or desired, or punished? What would our lives be like? Or rather, what would our relationships be like? How long would they last? What would people be doing together?

We might find ourselves saying things like: the cruelest thing one can do to one's partner is to be good at fidelity but bad at celebration. Or, people have affairs either because they're not praised enough by their partners, or because they are not praised in the way they most like. Or, it's not difficult to sustain a relationship but it's impossible to keep a celebration going. The long applause becomes baffling.

FOR the monogamist the thought of an infidelity is a secular equivalent of the afterlife. It is the thought of something infinitely better or infinitely worse: something, perhaps, one has to earn; a blackmail of sorts. Certainly something for the future.

But then what no one ever dared think about the afterlife was that it might be exactly the same as this one.

RULES are ways of imagining what to do. Our personal infidelity rituals – the choreography of our affairs – are the parallel texts of our 'marriages'. Guilt, by reminding us what we mustn't do shows us what we may want; it shows us our moral sense, the difference between what we want, and what we want to want. Without the possibility of a double life there is no morality.

IT'S impossible not to communicate. You cannot be for it or against it. You can only do it more or less well – by your own standards or by other people's – but you can't not do it.

In this sense, monogamy is like communication. It is as absurd to be against it as it is to be committed to it. Because we are always being sexually faithful to somebody, every preference is a betrayal. We are always doing monogamy, even though it is not always obvious with whom we are doing it.

WE can never be quite sure whether we are competing for something that doesn't exist, or winning a competition in which no one else is competing. This is why in marriage we are never quite sure who the joke is on. Nothing defeats us like success. It is always more baffling – more essentially ironic – than failure.

IF I believe that my partners' freedom entails my frustration, then my only freedom is to rob them of their freedom. This is the *folie à deux* of fidelity.

If I believe that my partners' freedom entails my own freedom, then the idea of permission disappears. This is the *folie à deux* of infidelity.

OUR erotic life is an attempt to make a politics that is too good for the world. But a politics that is too good for the world is a contradiction in terms. At least that is the news the world keeps sending someone to tell us. The breathless messenger keeps arriving, the eternal third party.

JEALOUSY and passion may be inextricable – each a sure sign of the other – and yet jealousy can outlast desire. Our appetites may be fickle but our sense of entitlement persists. This is the legacy of childhood: having your cake just in case you want to eat it.

But the having comes first. Without the certainty of possession there is only tantalisation and its more or less hopeless solutions: self-sufficiency, abolition of desire, fear of passion, hatred of sex, resentment, a life of hints and accusations. And yet, of course, there never was any certain possession, desire has never come with a guarantee. We have always been dependent on others for our well-being, which was never, could never, be their exclusive priority. The wish to own someone – or the belief that one does – is an acknowledgement of its impossibility; all sex crimes are a refusal of this fundamental recognition, a picture of how unbearable it might be.

But if jealousy is the way I notice that the other person is not my sole possession – not my thing – then I need to be betrayed to break out of the magic circle of myself. While betrayal makes us too real to each other, its impossibility makes us invisible.

SERIAL monogamy is a question not so much of quantity as of quality; a question not of how many, but of the order; of how the plot hangs together. Of what kind of person seems to be telling the story.

WHAT would we do without the idea of the Real Thing, the 'real' relationship? We would have to compare everything with everything else. Monogamy saves us from – and, alas, saves us for – the madness of comparisons. It domesticates the infinite.

THE outlaw, the femme fatale, the heretic, the double agent, the pun – infidelity gets all the action. It has the glamour of the bad secret and the good lie. It travels because it has to, because it believes in elsewhere.

So what would we have to do to make monogamy glamorous? Or rather, what would we have to stop doing?

THERE is no such thing as sexual competition, there is only the continual coming to terms with the fact that one can never be someone else to one's partner, that we are so quickly typecast in our relationships. Our rivals are merely other people. They are helpless, like us, because they only have one real advantage over us, and it is always decisive. They will never *be* us.

THE secure couple, satisfied and assured by each other, is one of our formative pictures of a good life, just as the unhappy couple represent our sense of the impossibility of happiness. As children we have all witnessed our parents' drama, and how much hung on it.

Our belief in the couple – in good couplings – is a measure of our sense of hope. After all, our conception, at least, was a monogamous moment, even if our first love affair was with someone who was 'married'.

MOST infidelities aren't ugly, they just look as though they are.

THERE are fundamentally two kinds of writer, just as there are two kinds of monogamist: the immaculate and the fallible. For the immaculate every sentence must be perfect, every word the inevitable one. For them, getting it right is the point. For the fallible, 'wrong' is only the word for people who need to be right. The fallible, that is to say, have the courage of their gaucheness; they are never quite sure what might be a good line; and they have a superstitious confidence that the bad lines somehow sponsor the good ones.

THE point about trust is that it is impossible to establish. It is a risk masquerading as a promise. The question is not, do you trust your partner? But do you know what they think trust is? And how would you go about finding out? And what might make you believe them? And what would make you trust your belief?

Trust is a word we have to put too much trust in.

IN our erotic lives we never do anything by halves. So to say that someone is possessive of their partner is never quite right because couples always are each other. This is why no one ever really separates from anybody. And also, of course, why people are never quite together.

SELF-BETRAYAL is a sentimental melodrama; a deification of our own better judgement, an adoration of shame. I am always true to myself, that is the problem. Who else could I be true to?

When I say that I have let myself down I am boasting. I am the only person I cannot avoid being faithful to. My sexual relationship with myself, in other words, is a study in monogamy.

IT is often easier to get other people to do what one wants than to get oneself to. So it's often the person in the couple who isn't having the affair that wants to, and the one that is that is bitterly unhappy.

We delegate more in our erotic lives than anywhere else. Someone has to do the dirty work.

IN our erotic life work does not work. This is its relief and its terror. It is no more possible to work at a relationship than it is to will an erection, or arrange to have a dream. In fact when you are working at it you know it has gone wrong, that something is already missing. In our erotic lives, in other words, trying is always trying too hard; we have to become lazy again about effort, because the good things only come when it stops – affection, curiosity, desire, unworrying attention.

Sexual relationships are only for the work-shy, because they do not work. They just give us more or less pleasure, more or less hope.

WE need to find a way of thinking about things that is not just a way of thinking of alternatives to them. We need to find the perfect partner.

IT is always flattering when a married person wants to have an affair with us; though we cannot help wondering exactly what will be compared with what. In fact, we become merely a comparison, just a good or a bad imitation.

To resent this would be to believe that we could ever be anything else.

NO one gets the relationship they deserve. For some people this is a cause of unending resentment, for some people it is the source of unending desire. And for some people the most important thing is that they have found something that doesn't end.

MONOGAMY and infidelity: two unfertility rituals, two traditional forms of contraception that we have never had total confidence in.

THE best hideout – the cosiest one – is the one in which you can forget what you are hiding from; or that you are hiding at all. The secret the couple have to keep – mostly from each other – is what they are hiding from and that they are hiding. The belief they have to sustain is that their fears are the same.

We have couples because it is impossible to hide alone.

WE need to replace the idea of the 'real' relationship with the idea of the pleasurable relationship.

But how then will we judge the promiscuous, if not by assuming that they are not really having pleasure?

THERE is always someone else who would love me more, understand me better, make me feel more sexually alive. This is the best justification we have for monogamy – and infidelity.

THE compulsive monogamist is like the compulsive libertine. For both of them something is too extravagant. For both of them there is a catastrophe to be averted. Monogamists are terrorised by their promiscuous wishes, libertines by their dependence. It is all a question of which catastrophe one prefers.

ABOUT pleasure we are all mystics. We are all ter-
rified of suffering from too much of it. For some
people the best solution to this is infidelity, for others
monogamy. To each his own asceticism.

BECAUSE erotic life rearranges the world it is political. Every form of erotic life makes a world. Our monogamies, our infidelities, our promiscuity go on in a world of other people, and cannot help but make a difference to the ways they organise their lives. Every infidelity creates the need for an election; every separation divides the party.

And yet we never wonder what kind of political thoughts monogamists are likely to have; or, how those committed to infidelity – or to sharing partners – would like to organise themselves as a group. How do the promiscuous tend to vote? When it comes to sexuality we seem to forget that privacy can only go on in public.

INFIDELITY makes a life of absolute monogamy essential.

MORE has been written about how relationships don't work, than about how they do. We have virtually no language, other than banality, to describe the couple who have been happy together for a long time. We would like them to have a secret, we would like them to have something they could give us. Or that we could give them, other than our suspicion.

There is nothing more terrorising than the possibility that nothing is hidden. There's nothing more scandalous than a happy marriage.

BABIES tell us nothing about infancy because they can't speak. And our beginning, of course, like all beginnings, tells us nothing inevitable or predictable about our middle or our end. Monogamy as our beginning and our end is too wishfully neat, too symmetrical for the proper mess that a life is.

But if monogamy *is* where we start from, our first knowledge is of infidelity; that is what knowledge is about. Temporarily the mother can be everything to the child, but the child cannot possibly be everything for the mother. He can't feed her or sexually satisfy her, or have adult conversations with her. From the child's dawning point of view the mother is – as the father will soon be – a model of promiscuity. She has a thousand things to do. She knows other people.

Small children, like uxorious husbands, are the most devoted of partners to their parents (they like coming with them to the toilet). Their parents, however, libertine if only in their responsibilities, have other commitments. Small children understand monogamy. Adults often find it daunting, even beyond them.

WHY is anthropology – at least for most people – essentially the study of different sexual customs? Because we want to be reassured that it's only possible to do it differently somewhere else.

A sexual relationship is like learning a script neither of you have read. But you only notice this when one of you forgets your lines. And then, in the panic, you desperately try and remember something that you haven't really forgotten. You hope the other person will prompt you. You start to hear voices off. You bring in another character.

ABOUT monogamy we would like to think that the sexes are different. That one sex is more moralistic, more conventional, more daring, more secretive, more lustful, and so on. We'd like a neat division of labour, a bit of reassuring biology, some huffy, inspiring religion; even some enthralling psychology, perhaps. Anything just to get it off our hands.

REALISTS love compromise, especially the realists of the erotic life. It means they can get a bit of sacrifice with their pleasure. Or rather, they can get another kind of pleasure with their pleasure.

IF we could find a cure for sexual jealousy – perhaps a drug – what would we not be capable of?

We would certainly have to rethink our ideas about progress. Or, at the very least, our ideas about progress in the arts.

YOU can be occasionally unfaithful, but you can't be occasionally monogamous. You can't be monogamous and unfaithful at the same time; you can't not be either. It's a double life each way. If you choose one, you choose the possibility of both. That's real commitment.

EACH of our relationships is different, and we are different in each of them. This is what makes monogamy so perversely interesting.

THERE are people, as we know, who can only be sexually aroused by the presence of a particular object: a shoe, a piece of clothing, a particular smile are the preconditions for their desire.

Of course, we prefer to think that it is the person who excites us; that we don't need to lay down these absurd conditions. That we follow our desire, or our moral sense, or our intuitions, when we are drawn to someone. And yet the fetish most people need is often simply the name of the relationship, its official title. The problem – or, indeed the pleasure – of a marriage is that it can never be called an affair. If the word doesn't fit then the genitals won't either.

THE most difficult task for every couple is to get the right amount of misunderstanding. Too little and you assume you know each other. Too much, and you begin to believe there must be someone else, somewhere, who does understand you.

We have affairs when we get our proportions wrong.

WE can be morally satisfied by someone who forgives us, but can we be sexually satisfied? One of the risks of monogamy is that it becomes confessional, and then we can't tell the difference.

WE begin to feel safe – a little uneasy, perhaps, but safe – when a new relationship begins to change into a familiar one. When we have settled into our routines, when all the false notes and small misunderstandings have become part of a larger understanding that we call our life together. We don't need to think about it – or think about it like this – we just enjoy each other's company. We cannot imagine ourselves without each other. And when we cannot imagine ourselves without each other, we are no longer together.

JUST as there are only two kinds of relationship – the official and the unofficial – there are also only two kinds of selves, the old and the new. Guilt gives us time to notice the differences between them, but neither of them really exists for long enough for us to easily tell them apart.

WE only really value a relationship when it sur-
vives our best attempts to destroy it. As every
sado-masochist knows, nothing is more seductive
than resilience. It is the only aphrodisiac that con-
tinues to work the more you take it. So the only way
we can test our infidelity is through monogamy. A lot
of confusion is created by our belief that it is the other
way round.

OUR children are the people we have, as it were, monogamous affairs with. We treat them as both lovers and partners, the forbidden and the familiar; as the people we will never leave, and as the people who will have to leave us. The people who we desire, and to whom we must be forever unfaithful. The people we can only love well by frustrating.

It is not that children spoil their parents' relationship, but that they confuse it. They blur our categories, which is why parents are so bossy. What else can you do with people who keep showing us the rules by breaking them, who keep exposing our prejudices by making us spell them out?

EVERYTHING we say is an experiment because we can never be quite sure how people will react, or how we ourselves will react. This is why people used to get engaged first.

SINCE the second half of the nineteenth century a lot of people have become agnostic about monogamy. They are really not sure whether it exists, or where it will all end if we no longer believe in it. If God is dead everything may be permitted, but if monogamy is dead what is to be done?

As least religious atheists could believe that God was dead, but what can the erotic atheist believe?

THERE is comfort in danger. This is the truth that the monogamist dreads, and the unfaithful rarely let themselves notice.

ONE is never cured of anything, one's preoccupations just change. Certain thoughts simply disappear without telling us. Similarly, one is truly monogamous only when monogamy is no longer the point: that is, when one is in love.

Being in love solves the problem of monogamy by making it irrelevant. Or rather, it solves the problem of one's own monogamy. When I am in love, it is only the other person who could be unfaithful. Even if I commit an unfaithful act – which, curiously, I am now freer to do – it will be innocent, harmless, without meaning. I become, at last, the absolute monogamist. The former vagrancy of my own desire is unthinkable.

With the most intense pleasure – in other words, conviction – I speak my love, and I am clearly believed. And yet, I am never sufficiently persuasive to convince myself that the other is faithful. Monogamy, I discover, is a religion of one.

COUPLEDOM is a sustained resistance to the
intrusion of third parties. The couple needs to
sustain the third parties in order to go on resisting
them. The faithful keep an eye on the enemy, eye
them up. After all, what would they do together if no
one else was there? How would they know what to
do?

Two's company, but three's a couple.

ALL prophets of the erotic life are false prophets because every couple has to invent sex for itself. They are not so much making love as making it up. In our erotic lives uncertainty is delight, our awkwardness is passion.

Only the cynic knows the future because he has seen it all before. For the omniscient sex is always a problem.

ONE of the most striking things about reading
stories to young children is the ruthless promiscuity of their attention. One minute they are utterly
absorbed in the adult's virtuoso performance, the next
moment a pigeon flies past the window and they are
off looking for it. At that moment it is as though there
was no story, no special or exclusive connection
between the two of you. You will feel impatient, or
outraged, or dismayed, or even exploited; in other
words, abandoned.

Two minutes later the child will come back as though
nothing has happened, or dragging another book that
will or won't hold their attention. The mobility of the
child's interest complicates our ideas about what it is
to be interesting. Young children relish the next best
thing. But the primitive art of losing interest in things
or people is itself easily lost. Good manners are the
best way of pretending that this is not an issue, that
we can make our feelings last, that our attention is
reliable.

Children drop adults far more than adults drop children. It is not that children haven't, as we say, learned
to concentrate, or are inept at commitment; but that
curiosity is not monogamous. It ranges. But the

waywardness of their attention soon becomes risky for children. Anything too intriguing, anything that makes them feel too alive, entails a conflict of loyalties. The best thing we can learn from children is how to lose interest. The worst thing they learn from adults is how to force their attention.

WE want to be the same as we are and we are always becoming different. We have to deceive ourselves better than anyone else because the infidelity we fear most is change. We are ahead of ourselves with our eyes closed; as though death is waiting there to let us down.

So when we commit ourselves to anyone we are being imperious with time, absurdly possessive of it. To behave like this you have to be convinced of something.

THE opposite of monogamy is not just promiscuity, but the absence or the impossibility of relationship itself. Indeed, one reason monogamy is so important to us is because we are so terrorised by what we imagine are the alternatives to it. The other person we fear most is the one who does not believe in the universal sacrality of – usually heterosexual – coupledom. As homophobia, xenophobia, all the phobias tell us: if we don't choose monogamy our fate will be isolation or the chaos of impersonality. A threat, that is to say, not a promise.

Abandonment and exclusion, or getting too mixed up with, and by, other people. In unguarded circulation, or stranded. In other words, we do not know whether we want monogamy, but we do know that we fear excess: an excess of solitude and an excess of company. We are not, of course, naturally monogamous. We are the animals for whom something is too much.

IT is always a temptation to see how bad one can be, but only to find out how good one is at being bad. Don Juan was nothing if not conscientious.

OUR survival depends upon our realising the difference between the One and the Many. We may
begin our lives being fed by one person, but we soon
notice that various people can do it for us and, indeed,
that we can do it for ourselves. Adaptation is the
polite word for promiscuity. We need a certain versat-
ility where appetite is concerned. We need to be able
to use what is there; to make of scavenging a
romance.

It is not that one person cannot satisfy all our needs,
but that with each person we create a new set of
needs. This is one way we can tell that we have found
a new person. Couples make appetites together; this is
the calling of coupledom. Each new person shows us
that there is something else to want, but usually in the
guise of someone else to want. Seduction, the happy
invention of need.

MASTURBATION is traditionally taboo not because it damages your health – it is not only safe sex, it is safe incest – or because it is against the law, but because we fear it may be the truth about sex: that sex is something we do on our own. That our lovers are just a prompt or a hint there to remind us of our own erotic delirium, the people who connect us to somewhere else. People, that is to say, who are gods and godesses in spite of themselves; because as people our lovers are too complicated to excite us. The erotic is a simplification.

So why do we, at least apparently, have sex with other people, why include them at all? If masturbation is about having it the way you want it, sex with other people is about having it the way you didn't know you wanted it. Other people are something else. The virtue of monogamy is the ease with which it can turn sex into masturbation; the vice of monogamy is that it gives you nothing else. If two can be one too many, so can one be.

When we masturbate, it goes without saying, we are always having sex with ourselves. There is no suggestion of infidelity, except in a sense to our partner. Even if masturbation is the way we discover intense erotic excitement, our masturbation fantasies are strikingly repetitive and uninventive. They are as embarrassing to tell as they are dull to listen to. Masturbation, like monogamy, doesn't usually make a good story. But then monogamy is the bidden thing.

Our commitment to monogamy depends upon our appetite for good stories. And on our appetite for appetite. The only truly monogamous relationship is the one we have with ourselves.

THE climax of monogamy is separation. The climax of infidelity is monogamy. It is always the end that gets in the way. Climaxes are the worst kind of interruption.

But then without interruption we wouldn't know what was going on. Habit closes our eyes. In the erotic life it is important, above all, not to confuse our aims with our ends.

IF a law was passed saying that no one was allowed to be monogamous for more than three weeks people would feel under terrible pressure. But pressure to do what exactly? Why would they be suffering? What would they feel deprived of? What would their banners say when they took to the streets?

NOT everything turns into its opposite because not everything has an opposite. Contradiction is the foreplay of logicians. So if infidelity and monogamy don't lead to each other, where else can they go?

We would prefer our alternatives to be opposites. It narrows the field, by making a path.

THE fact that jealousy sustains desire – or at least kindles it – suggests how precarious desire is. Not only do we need to find a partner, we also need to find a rival. And not only do we have to tell them apart, we also have to keep them apart. We need our rivals to tell us who our partners are. We need our partners to help us find rivals.

We need so many people to make desire work, to make it desirable. No wonder we are always trying to keep the numbers down.

THE questions for the couple are: do they want to use each other to sustain their desire, or to finish with it? And is their desire more important than their desire for each other? The drama of these larger questions usually turns up as the melodrama of a smaller question: is sex that important? With this question – so much more abstract and reassuring – the couple can rejoin the comforting world of research and questionnaires. The world of all those answers.

MOST people would never have engaged in
monogamy if they had never heard monogamy
spoken of.

IT is a poorly kept secret – certainly not something one enjoys witnessing – that couples are extremely competitive with each other. But then seducing a rival is far more difficult – more of a challenge so to speak – than seducing an ally. The rival always resists. Perhaps, then, one can only seduce a rival? Perhaps seduction is just a cure for competition?

WHAT happens when couples 'rediscover' each other – one of the few, if minor, redemptions that are possible in time? Is it like a brief affair with someone, delightful because they know it has to end? Or an act of defiance against the regime of time, like a revolution in manners? Or the secular grace that sustains our belief in frustration?

These unprompted renewals are proof, if we needed it, that we can only allow people to be different in small doses. That we want to know everything in order to be proved wrong.

THE things about people that we fall in love with are often the things that end up driving us mad. Either we cannot bear the intensity of our love, or we didn't really love these things in the first place – they were merely what required some psychic alchemy to make something else possible. It is this something else that really fascinates us, that keeps us together.

This is what makes relationships last: the disillusionment that is the key to a life-long romance.

FAMILIARITY may increase our affection, our respect, even our time for other people, but it rarely increases our desire for them (indeed, the attempt to value affection over desire is one of the good – one of the underestimated – aims of monogamy). Continuity reassures us, but it also unsexes us, which may be part of its appeal. Strangeness is exciting but it threatens to derange us; routine is comforting but it threatens to put us to sleep. Nothing convinces us of our capacity to make choices – nothing sustains our illusion of freedom – more than our ability to regularise our behaviour. And nothing is more capable of destroying our interest and our pleasure in what we do.

If it is the predictable that stupefies us and the unpredictable that terrorises us, what should we do? If we are always caught between risk and resignation, between confidence and catastrophe, how can we decide what to do next? Perhaps we should remember, before we take flight into grand ideas about human nature – or even worse, the human condition – that there is a difference between having something because you want it, and wanting it because you have it.

THE hardest thing to give up is our habit of making things we have to give in to. We speak of giving in to a temptation, as though we have submitted to something, rather than made something to submit to. We speak of deferring to someone else's judgement, but not of choosing the people we defer to. We have to continually remind ourselves that our vices are as much our invention as our virtues. That we never lose control, we just sometimes break the rules. That we are not entirely unfaithful, we are just faithful to something else.

We are more interested in the rule we have broken than the rule we abide by when we break it. As long as we are addicted to punishment and to blame, and not to the alternatives, we will never get the full story. Only the old story.

IT may be purgatory to be left out but it is hell to be left in. As every child knows who has watched his parents kiss – or indeed, who has suffered the consummate betrayal of their sleeping together – when you are excluded you can do something (you can imagine what it would be like if you weren't). But if they invited you in where would you start? How could you participate? It is a terrible deprivation for the adults to exclude the children from feeling left out; but it is a terrible deception to pretend it is possible to protect them from feeling left out. There can be no life without violence because all violence is the violence of exclusion.

Because everyone has had the experience of being left out – everyone, in other words, has been a child – everyone has an imagination (a provocation is also an invitation). You figure out how to get in, or you figure out what else there is. Because we are redundant we have to find something other to do; or do something with the experience of being left out, like finding someone we can make envious. We are so glued, or appalled, by people kissing because it is a revelation of our irrelevance (not to mention their need to make someone else feel invisible). Where we go is where we go from there. Our life will be what we can make of feeling left out. That experience, which takes so many forms, is the raw material.

Imagination, then, is the comforting word for sexual jealousy; ambition, the slightly less comforting word; and obsession . . .? Obsession signifies the triumph of the couple who exclude us, our determined or helpless poverty in the face of our exclusion. Obsession is a way of dispelling alternatives, an abrogation of choice, a cure for thought. If it speaks, somehow, of our unwillingness to leave home, our first and necessary obsession, it also speaks of our fear of freedom. Which is partly, of course, our freedom to leave other people out.

HOW can we be unacceptable to ourselves? For some people, of course, the question is, what else can we be? In fact, to ask the question at all is to be already condemned, if only to callous naïvety. It could not be more obvious that we are not as good as we ought to be. But from whose point of view?

The question is slightly less ludicrous once we realise that we have to learn to be unacceptable to ourselves. It doesn't come easily. Babies don't steal, they just grab the things that interest them. They are not pissing on their mothers, they are just pissing. We learn to feel guilty and ashamed in, or from, a couple. At the so-called beginning couples are people who, among other things, have to say no. They make us feel better by making us feel bad.

This is the puzzle of coupledom that we take from the couple we find ourselves in as children, to the couples we make as adults: can we be protected without there being a protection racket?

ONE way of loving people is to acknowledge that they have desires which exclude us; that it is possible to love and desire more than one person at the same time. Everyone knows that this is true, and yet we don't want the people we love to start believing it about themselves.

We reserve our most generous, our most ennobling love for ourselves. After all, other people might abuse it. I am free to leave out the people I love, but they must never leave me out unless I want them to. I have a right to be unfaithful, they have an obligation not to be. I love the people I happen to love, but no one I love is allowed to do that.

Unfortunately, I am so busy keeping an eye on the people I love that I have no time to be free. That is, I believe in my freedom but I don't seem to want it.

E VERYBODY, one might say, is left out of being someone else. But that is no comfort. Coupledom is as close as you can get.

O NE of the commonest solutions to the pervasive problem of our own envy – which can be our best, our most dismaying clue to what we want – is to make ourselves enviable. This means that the couple who need to be enviable rather than to just enjoy themselves never want each other, because they never know what they want. If the audience sustains the couple, then the couple must be faithful to the audience.

FROM time to time every couple believes either that they are too good for each other, or that they are not good enough. The problem is not whether it is true, but how it could ever be decided. Who would be in a position to judge?

This is where third parties can be so helpful: for arbitration, as it were, or as referees. But they can only *play* this role, of course, because they are never impartial.

IN a society without scapegoats there would be more conflict. People feel too vulnerable without someone else to blame and punish. Similarly, a society without sexual infidelity – or without the promiscuous going their wanton way – could be dangerous. Who would we be fascinated by, who would we persecute?

After all, a couple without a third party are radically unprotected from each other. And when people are unprotected from each other it can go either way.

WE are never misunderstood we are just sometimes understood in ways we don't like. We
are never unfaithful, we are just sometimes faithful in
ways we don't like.

MONOGAMY and infidelity: the difference between making a promise and being promising.